حمن الرحيم

الله
رسول
محمد

About The Author

The author, who writes under the pen-name HARUN YAHYA, was born in Ankara in 1956. Having completed his primary and secondary education in Ankara, he then studied arts at Istanbul's Mimar Sinan University and philosophy at Istanbul University. Since the 1980s, the author has published many books on political, faith-related and scientific issues. Harun Yahya is well-known as an author who has written very important works disclosing the imposture of evolutionists, the invalidity of their claims and the dark liaisons between Darwinism and bloody ideologies such as fascism and communism.

His pen-name is made up of the names "Harun" (Aaron) and "Yahya" (John), in memory of the two esteemed prophets who fought against lack of faith. The Prophet's seal on the cover of the books is symbolic and is linked to the their contents. It represents the Qur'an (the final scripture) and the Prophet Muhammad, the last of the prophets. Under the guidance of the Qur'an and sunnah, the author makes it his purpose to disprove each one of the fundamental tenets of godless ideologies and to have the "last word", so as to completely silence the objections raised against religion. The seal of the final Prophet, who attained ultimate wisdom and moral perfection, is used as a sign of his intention of saying this last word.

All author's works center around one goal: to convey the Qur'an's message to people, encourage them to think about basic faith-related issues (such as the existence of Allah, His unity and the Hereafter), and to expose the feeble foundations and perverted ideologies of godless systems.

Harun Yahya enjoys a wide readership in many countries, from India to America, England to Indonesia, Poland to Bosnia, and Spain to Brazil. Some of his books are available in English, French, German, Spanish, Italian, Portuguese, Urdu, Arabic, Albanian, Russian, Serbo-Croat (Bosnian), Polish, Malay, Uygur Turkish, and Indonesian, and they are enjoyed by readers worldwide.

Greatly appreciated all around the world, these works have been instrumental in many people recovering their faith in Allah and in many others gaining a deeper insight into their faith. The wisdom, and the sincere and easy-to-understand style gives these books a distinct touch which directly effects any one who reads or studies them. Immune to objections, these works are characterized by their features of rapid effectiveness, definite results and irrefutability. It is unlikely that those who read these books and give serious thought to them can any longer sincerely advocate the materialistic philosophy, atheism or any other perverted ideology or philosophy. Even if they continue to do so, it will be only a sentimental insistence since these books refuted such ideologies from their very foundations. All contemporary movements of denial are now ideologically defeated, thanks to the collection of books written by Harun Yahya.

There is no doubt that these features result from the wisdom and lucidity of the Qur'an. The author modestly intends to serve as a means in humanity's search for Allah's right path. No material gain is sought in the publication of these works.

Considering these facts, those who encourage people to read these books, which open the "eyes" of the heart and guide them to become more devoted servants of Allah, render an invaluable service.

Meanwhile, it would just be a waste of time and energy to propagate other books which create confusion in peoples' minds, lead man into ideological chaos, and which, clearly have no strong and precise effects in removing the doubts in peoples' hearts, as also verified from previous experience. It is apparent that it is impossible for books devised to emphasize the author's literary power rather than the noble goal of saving people from loss of faith, to have such a great effect. Those who doubt this can readily see that the sole aim of Harun Yahya's books is to overcome disbelief and to disseminate the moral values of the Qur'an. The success and impact of this service are manifest in readers' conviction.

One point should be kept in mind: The main reason for the continuing cruelty, conflict, and all the ordeals the majority of people undergo is the ideological prevalence of disbelief. This state can only be ended with the ideological defeat of disbelief and by conveying the wonders of creation and Qur'anic morality so that people can live by it. Considering the state of the world today, which leads people into the downward spiral of violence, corruption and conflict, it is clear that this service has to be provided more speedily and effectively. Otherwise, it may be too late.

It is no exaggeration to say that the collection of books by Harun Yahya have assumed this leading role. By the will of Allah, these books will be a means through which people in the 21st century will attain the peace, justice and happiness promised in the Qur'an.

The works of the author include *The New Masonic Order, Judaism and Freemasonry, Global Freemasonry, Kabbalah and Freemasonry, Knight Templars, Islam Denounces Terrorism, Terrorism: The Ritual of the Devil, The Disasters Darwinism Brought to Humanity, Communism in Ambush, Fascism: The Bloody Ideology of Darwinism, The 'Secret Hand' in Bosnia, Behind the Scenes of The Holocaust, Behind the Scenes of Terrorism, Israel's Kurdish Card, The Oppression Policy of Communist China and Eastern Turkestan, Palestine, Solution: The Values of the Qur'an, The Winter of Islam and Its Expected Spring, Articles 1-2-3, A Weapon of Satan: Romanticism, The Light of the Qur'an Destroyed Satanism, Signs from the Chapter of the Cave to the Last Times, Signs of the Last Day, The Last Times and The Beast of the Earth, Truths 1-2, The Western World Turns to God, The Evolution Deceit, Precise Answers to Evolutionists, The Blunders of Evolutionists, Confessions of Evolutionists, The Misconception of the Evolution of the Species, The Qur'an Denies Darwinism, Perished Nations, For Men of Understanding, The Prophet Musa, The Prophet Yusuf, The Prophet Muhammad (saas), The Prophet Sulayman, The Golden Age, Allah's Artistry in Colour, Glory is Everywhere, The Importance of the Evidences of Creation, The Truth of the Life of This World, The Nightmare of Disbelief, Knowing the Truth, Eternity Has Already Begun, Timelessness and the Reality of Fate, Matter: Another Name for Illusion, The Little Man in the Tower, Islam and the Philosophy of Karma, The Dark Magic of Darwinism, The Religion of Darwinism, The Collapse of the Theory of Evolution in 20 Questions, Engineering in Nature, Technology Mimics Nature, The Impasse of Evolution I (Encyclopedic), The Impasse of Evolution II (Encyclopedic), Allah is Known Through Reason, The Qur'an Leads the Way to Science, The Real Origin of Life, Consciousness in the Cell, Technology Imitates Nature, A String of Miracles, The Creation of the Universe, Miracles of the Qur'an, The Design in Nature, Self-Sacrifice and Intelligent Behaviour Models in Animals, The End of Darwinism, Deep Thinking, Never Plead Ignorance, The Green Miracle: Photosynthesis, The Miracle in the Cell, The Miracle in the Eye, The Miracle in the Spider, The Miracle in the Gnat, The Miracle in the Ant, The Miracle of the Immune System, The Miracle of Creation in Plants, The Miracle in the Atom, The Miracle in the Honeybee, The Miracle of Seed, The Miracle of Hormone, The Miracle of the Termite, The Miracle of the Human Body, The Miracle of Man's Creation, The Miracle of Protein, The Miracle of Smell and Taste, The Miracle of Microworld, The Secrets of DNA.*

The author's childrens books are: *Wonders of Allah's Creation, The World of Animals, The Glory in the Heavens, Wonderful Creatures, Let's Learn Our Islam, The Miracles in Our Bodies, The World of Our Little Friends: The Ants, Honeybees That Build Perfect Combs, Skillful Dam Builders: Beavers.*

The author's other works on Quranic topics include: *The Basic Concepts in the Qur'an, The Moral Values of the Qur'an, Quick Grasp of Faith 1-2-3, Ever Thought About the Truth?, Crude Understanding of Disbelief, Devoted to Allah, Abandoning the Society of Ignorance, The Real Home of Believers: Paradise, Knowledge of the Qur'an, Qur'an Index, Emigrating for the Cause of Allah, The Character of the Hypocrite in the Qur'an, The Secrets of the Hypocrite, The Names of Allah, Communicating the Message and Disputing in the Qur'an, Answers from the Qur'an, Death Resurrection Hell, The Struggle of the Messengers, The Avowed Enemy of Man: Satan, The Greatest Slander: Idolatry, The Religion of the Ignorant, The Arrogance of Satan, Prayer in the Qur'an, The Theory of Evolution, The Importance of Conscience in the Qur'an, The Day of Resurrection, Never Forget, Disregarded Judgements of the Qur'an, Human Characters in the Society of Ignorance, The Importance of Patience in the Qur'an, General Information from the Qur'an, The Mature Faith, Before You Regret, Our Messengers Say, The Mercy of Believers, The Fear of Allah, Jesus Will Return, Beauties Presented by the Qur'an for Life, A Bouquet of the Beauties of Allah 1-2-3-4, The Iniquity Called "Mockery," The Mystery of the Test, The True Wisdom According to the Qur'an, The Struggle Against the Religion of Irreligion, The School of Yusuf, The Alliance of the Good, Slanders Spread Against Muslims Throughout History, The Importance of Following the Good Word, Why Do You Deceive Yourself?, Islam: The Religion of Ease, Zeal and Enthusiasm Described in the Qur'an, Seeing Good in All, How do the Unwise Interpret the Qur'an?, Some Secrets of the Qur'an, The Courage of Believers, Being Hopeful in the Qur'an, Justice and Tolerance in the Qur'an, Basic Tenets of Islam, Those Who do not Listen to the Qur'an, Taking the Qur'an as a Guide, A Lurking Threat: Heedlessness, Sincerity in the Qur'an, The Religion of Worshipping People, The Methods of the Liar in the Qur'an.*

Goodword Books Pvt. Ltd.
1, Nizamuddin West Market
New Delhi 110 013
e-mail: info@goodwordbooks.com
www.goodwordbooks.com
www.harunyahya.org
Printed in India
First published in 2003
Reprinted 2005

SKILFUL DAM CONSTRUCTORS:

BEAVERS

HARUN YAHYA

Karim is the first character in our book. He enjoys playing sports, reading books and is very interested in animals. Thanks to the books he has read, he has learnt a lot about animals. He even knows things about animals that other people don't. He recognizes animals in pictures and knows their features very well. This is one of the reasons why his friends like Karim a lot. They enjoy chatting to him during breaks or on the way to and from school.

His parents know about Karim's interest in nature. So, they go on trips with him at weekends and on holidays when the weather is fine.

Of these trips, Karim especially enjoys the spring camp they go to every year, because very interesting things happen to him in this camp. He meets and makes friends with different people, and learns about fascinating creatures. As the camp time draws near, Karim gets excited about the surprising and adventurous experiences he will have in the camp this year.

Now let's see what happens to Karim in the camp, and meet the other characters.

First day of the spring camp

The first day of the camp is a bit busier than the following days because Karim's parents have to put up a tent and open up their luggage. By the time they finish all these jobs, it has got dark. So Karim has to wait until the next morning to see what his surroundings are like.

The next morning, Karim gets up early and wakes his father and they set out together to explore the camp, which Karim has not been to before. There are huge trees everywhere. Behind the trees is a burbling river with very beautiful and colourful flowers on its banks.

Karim is thrilled to hear the sound of the running water which almost drowns out the chirping and twittering songs of the birds. The view he sees fills him with admiration and they spend some time there. But it's getting late, and his father tells him it's time to return to the camp, so they turn back.

Karim tells his sister, brother and mother about the magnificent view and the river they saw. They say they would also like to go with him the next day. They have been curious to know where that loud sound was coming from.

The following day, Karim, and his sister and brother set out to explore the area. When they come to the river bank, Karim realizes that several trees he saw the day before have been cut down . They have been carefully torn down and only the roots are left. As Karim wonders by whom and why these trees were felled, his sister calls out to him:

"Look Karim, there are logs in the water."

Karim is surprised. He wonders why someone would do such a thing. He cannot see anyone around either. After spending a little longer on the river bank, they get back to the camp.

Karim, his sister and brother go to the river bank on

the next few days, and become more and more curious because each day they find several more trees cut down and thrown into the water. Besides, the branches seem to have been carefully detached from the trees, and piled up on purpose with the logs. The loud sound of the river has been muffled now and a small pond is beginning to form. Karim has started to think that these things are not happening by chance. It is as if someone is working hard at the river bank every day and doing so with a purpose. So who is this mysterious person?

Karim makes a plan to satisfy his curiosity. He intends to go to the river bank very early, to find out who is doing all these things. He tells his brother about this and convinces him to come with him. The next morning, they carry out their plan.

You must be wondering what this pile of logs is doing in the water. So just continue reading. What you will learn will be both surprising and enjoyable.

Karim meets the mysterious strangers...

As they get closer to the river, Karim starts to walk on tiptoe. He sees that there are even more branches and logs in the water. He looks around and thinks that there is no one there at all. He is about to call out to his brother, when he suddenly sees two lovely animals floating on the water. He hides. Not having spotted Karim, the animals continue to work. Soon his brother, whose name is Imran, comes and whispers to Karim in astonishment: "So it was the beavers who cut down the trees and carried them into the water." Karim is so happy to see live beavers, which he has seen in books but has not known much about. They watch these two hard-working, interesting animals all day.

Karim's brother tells him that the beavers are trying to dam the water so as to build a home. The behaviour of beavers is astonishing. They place the branches they are carrying in their mouths in front of the largest log which they had previously dragged into the water. Then they come up on to the bank and head towards a nearby tree. One of the beavers first feeds on the leaves of the tree, then starts to gnaw the tree bark with its teeth. It gnaws

12

From behind the trees, Karim and Imran watch the lovable beavers and the amazing task they continue to carry out, unaware they are being watched.

the wood around the tree trunk, equally from each side. It keeps doing this until the breaking point of the tree looks like a sharpened pencil.

As the beaver gnaws the tree trunk, Karim wonders how this small animal will carry the huge tree. At that very moment, the tree falls into the water, solving the problem of how it will be carried.

Then the other beaver comes and starts to gnaw a

tree, which, again, directly falls into the water. Then another, then another, then another... All the trees which the beavers cut down break and fall into the water. It is as if the beavers start gnawing the trees after making calculations to ensure that they will fall into the water.

Karim is surprised because he had not thought of such a way of avoiding carrying the trees. He tells Imran what he thinks and finds that he is of the same opinion:

Before setting about working, beavers feed on the leaves they have collected, and this gives them energy.

In the next page, you see the trees cut down by beavers. Never forget that these small animals which chop down huge trees act by the inspiration of Allah.

Imran: To be honest, I couldn't think of how to do it either. But I read about it once. Beavers calculate how to make the tree fall into the water and gnaw the tree at a particular angle. But when they fail, as they sometimes do, they drag the tree into the water with their teeth. Karim, I think this is enough for today. Would you like me to tell you more about beavers when we get back to the camp? We could read about them if you want.

Karim: Yes, I'd love to do that. I am amazed at how beavers can make such calculations and act so intelligently. It is also confusing. Why do they dam the river to build a home? Don't their teeth wear out with eating bark? I've got lots of questions about this. I could talk about them all night.

Imran: OK, but we must return to the camp now. We've lost track of the time chatting, and it's almost dark. Let's go back before mom starms worrying about us. Besides, I feel sleepy and tired. Come on, hurry up.

They hurry back to the camp in a rush. However,

questions keep crossing Karim's mind on the way. Once they are back in the camp, they eat the delicious meal their mother has prepared for them. Then they look up beavers in their books. But Karim realizes that Imran has fallen asleep. So Karim starts to read on his own.

This leaves Karim alone with the questions on his mind. So he makes a new plan. He will meet the beavers the next morning and will learn from them what they do. Shortly after he falls asleep too...

When they fail to make the tree fall into the water, beavers drag the logs into the water with their teeth. In the above picture, you see Mr. Beaver dragging a tree.

A big surprise

Karim wakes up early in the morning and quietly goes to the river side. He finds the beavers working again. Mustering up courage, he approaches them and says:

"Hello, my name is Karim. Can I be friends with you?"

The animals are startled at first, but seeing Karim's friendly manner, the bigger one comes forward and replies:

"Of course, my name is Mr. Beaver. And this is my wife, Mrs. Beaver. Nice to meet you."

This makes Karim happy, because now he can ask them what he is curious about. So they start chatting.

Karim: I've been watching you curiously for some time now, and there are so many questions I want to ask you... Let's start with the tree trunks. Mr. Beaver, why do you drag the trunks into the water and place them on top of others?

Mr. Beaver: All beaver couples, like us, migrate to build new homes for themselves. We arrived here a short time ago, having recently moved to this river. Now we're building our home. But to do that, we need still water. So we have to block the water flow first. This is why we have piled up logs and formed this artificial pond.

21

Karim: So you are constructing a dam? This is great. You know what? We human beings have also constructed dams for centuries in the same way to block the water flow. The other day our geography teacher taught us the dams in our country and explained how they were constructed. It surprised me because I thought it must be very difficult to build a wall in front of running water. But what you are doing is even more amazing and difficult. How do you manage to block such a fast flowing river? How did you discover this method? Did you decide to do things in this way when you saw the man-made dams?...

In his excitement, Karim asks one question after another. His words and his astonishment make Mr. Beaver smile, because what they do is so easy for them that they don't give it a second thought.

Mr. Beaver: OK, Karim, take a breather. I'll answer your questions one by one. Don't worry, you'll learn everything. Our knowledge of how to construct dams and to build such homes comes naturally to us. Of course, this knowledge did not come to us by chance. It is not that one day we said, "Let's construct a dam and build a home in the water." We had already had this information, because it had been taught to us before we were born. Because of this, we know what to do very well and successfully do our jobs. Again thanks to this knowledge, we know how to fell huge trees and to carry them into the water.

Listening to Mr. Beaver in amazement, Karim is startled by Imran's voice behind him:

"I can answer all of your questions Karim. But before this, you owe me an explanation. Why did you leave the camp alone? We would have been worried about you if we had not seen your note.

Karim: Well, I... I'm so sorry. I was so excited that I couldn't help coming here. But I knew that you would see my note. Will you please tell me who taught the beavers all these things?

Imran: OK, Karim. You remember that we read the Qur'an together last week? Allah said in many verses that it was He Who created everything in the skies, on the earth and in between these two. We talked about the animals we knew and about their exceptional behaviour. Then we concluded that they could not do these things by themselves and had, in fact, been taught how to act by someone else.

Karim: Yes, I remember.

Imran: All living things act in the way Allah teaches them to. From the moment they are born, they all know how to behave. To understand their behaviour, we human beings make studies and carry out research for years on end; we use technological devices, read books and make experiments. But these things which we try hard to understand are easily done by animals. For example, they make calculations that would baffle even the experts. Mr. and Mrs. Beaver are doing what our Lord has taught them to do. If Mr. Beaver tells us more about what they do, you will understand what I mean much better.

Mr. Beaver: Yes, Karim. Soon I'll tell you in detail about the home we are building. You, too, will learn that it is not possible for us to do such a thing just by using our own intelligence.

Karim listens to Mr. Beaver and Imran carefully, because he is aware of the importance of this conversation. So he decides to concentrate on what they say and to ask about things he is eager to learn.

Karim: Mr. Beaver, I guess you use your paws and teeth to fell trees so as to form this pond. But how come your teeth are so strong? My teeth, for example, would break if I attempted to bite off a branch. I could never do that.

Mr. Beaver: Good question Karim. My wife and I can cut down about 400 trees in a year. We do this by gnawing with our teeth. We use the four front teeth to gnaw tree branches. Our teeth also, wear down not though as

nearly much as yours, and sometimes break. But this does not affect us, because our front teeth, called incisors, keep growing throughout our lives.

Karim: So your teeth keep growing, just like our nails do, right?

Mrs. Beaver: Let me answer your question Karim. Yes, you are right. Allah created our teeth differently from those of any other living thing. If He hadn't done so, we wouldn't be able to feed or build our homes, which would be too bad for us. Since the members of the species would starve to death, our species would eventually become extinct, that is, we would not be here today. You would not find even a single beaver on the face of the earth. However, my teeth, as well as Mr. Beaver's and all other beavers', grow very fast. As you can see, our teeth are vital to us.

Karim: OK. But how did you learn to swim? I've learnt

it recently. How come you are such perfect swimmers?

Mr. Beaver: Karim, all beavers can swim shortly after they are born. This is so easy for us, because our bodies are convenient for swimming. For one thing, our feet are webbed, so that we can easily push the water, and for another, our flat tails serve as flippers, so that we can move easily in the water. Just as you wear goggles to protect your eyes from the water and help you to see under water, we have natural goggles. And our ears and nostrils can close tightly to keep water out. We have three eyelids on each eye. One of them is semi-transparent, letting us see under water while also protecting our eyes from the hazards of the water.

Karim: My little friends, I, too, can swim fast and easily when I wear flippers on my feet. My father bought me the flippers, but you get yours at birth. Allah has created you with the exact features you need.

27

That is Allah, your Lord. There is no god
but Him, the Creator of everything.
So worship Him...
(Surat al-An'am: 102)

As well as the tail which serves as flippers (above), the paws, teeth, indeed, every single part of a beaver's body has been specially and perfectly created by our Lord. Without these features, beavers could not survive.

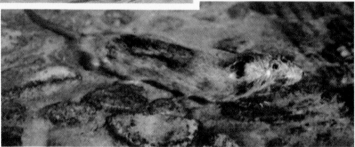

Imran: You are right, Karim. Mr. Beaver, will you please tell us a little about the dams you construct?

Mr. Beaver: First of all, we drag logs and branches on to the bed of the stream. Then we pile light branches up on the heavier ones. But we must place them firmly in position, otherwise the running water will take away what we build. That is why we add logs and strengthen the dam with rocks. But it is still not strong enough, so we need to support it. So we stick the branches together with a special mixture composed of mud and leaves. This waterproof mixture is also resistant to the eroding effect of the water.

Karim: If it wasn't the case, you would never be able to build a dry lodge under water. All your efforts would go to waste.

Mrs. Beaver: You're right, Karim. But the dam we

30

build is very strong and it becomes bigger and stronger every day. As the barrier gets larger, the level of the water collected before it rises. So after several months, a dam pond is formed. But as the pond becomes enlarged, we must strengthen and repair the dam. As Mr. Beaver said, we fill in the spaces between the branches with mud and bushes. By the way, there is one more thing which is very important. Have you noticed the shape of our dam? It looks like an arch, doesn't it?

Mr. Beaver explains to Karim how they carry the logs and branches into the water (page left) and then how Mrs. Beaver sticks them together.

These piled up branches will soon form the beavers' home.

While building their home, the beavers scurry about, bringing the small branches first of all. **Allah made these creatures very skilful and intelligent.**

Then the heavier pieces of wood and branches are brought by the hard-working beavers.

Beavers use mud in building their homes. They stick the branches and logs together with mud.

This shape which curves inwards is called concave. All beaver dams are constructed concavely. We aim to dam the water at an angle of 45 degrees.

Excited by what Mr. and Mrs. Beaver have told him, Karim interrupts:

Karim: How do you know that? We went on a trip to a dam with our teacher, and that day she told us that modern dams were constructed just like yours. They all curved inwards. She also told us that thanks to this

While Mrs. Beaver explains to Karim how they construct the dam...

shape, which was called concave, human beings could dam the water at an angle of exactly 45 degrees. Also concave dams, being the strongest are best able to withstand the water pressure. But how come you possess such knowledge, Mr. and Mrs. Beaver? Who taught you this? I know that dams are constructed by engineers. My sister is an engineer too; she had to have years of education before she could become an engineer. But you cannot go to school, so how come you know this? Did you find the correct knowledge by trial and error? Who taught you this knowledge?

What surprises Karim most is how beavers can construct a dam just like the ones humans do.

Karim watches Mr. and Mrs. Beaver with admiration and astonishment while they are gradually constructing the dam. He thinks, "How can they do this?"

Imran: Look Karim. It's quite impossible for the beaver family to carry out all these things in a random way. Do you remember that you once asked me about a person named Darwin? One of the books you read stated that animals came into being and acquired the characteristics they possess by chance. You found that to be nonsense and thought what Darwin said was a lie.

Karim: Yes, I remember. And I understand you very well. Mr. and Mrs. Beaver surely could not have learnt these things by chance. Darwin certainly lied.

Mr. Beaver: As I told you earlier, we know how to do all these things at birth. You are a very smart boy, Karim. Of course I've never gone to school. And it is not possible that I should have discovered these things by trial and error.

In the picture you can see Darwin, who lied and tried to deceive everyone. Karim is a very smart boy. Thanks to what Imran has told him and the books he has read, he immediately understands that Darwin was a liar.

If anyone comes up with such a nonsensical idea, you can just ask him these questions:

Even if we suppose that a beaver, say Mrs. Beaver or I, discovered how to build this lodge by coincidence, we see that all beavers build their homes in the same way. Have they all discovered it by coincidence?

As my teeth wear down, new ones grow in their place. This is the same for all beavers. Isn't it clear that this could not have come about as a result of coincidences?

As you can see, one merely needs to think a little to see how impossible this is and how senseless this claim is. Please ask your sister in which course they learnt that dams should be built at an angle of 45 degrees and what kinds of calculation they needed to make. Then you will understand me better.

Karim: You are right Mr. Beaver. It is evident that a Superior Being of outstanding intelligence taught you all these things. Mom told me that Allah is All-Wise. It is evidence of the matchless wisdom of our Lord that He taught this both to you and to other beavers as well as to all beavers who have lived so far. I know too that it is not only you whom Allah taught what to do, but all living things.

Imran: Yes, Karim. Allah creates all living things and has power over all things. As is stated in a verse of the Quran:

Allah created every animal from water. Some of them go on their bellies, some of them on two legs, and some on four. Allah creates whatever He wills. Allah has power over all things. (Surat an-Nur: 45)

The chat continues...

Karim: Mr. Beaver, you said that you construct the dam to build a home. But I cannot see anything that looks like a home. There is only a pile of logs. Where do you build your home?

Mr. Beaver: You are right. You cannot see our home from the outside. We build it like this on purpose so that it is a safe haven. While constructing the dam, we also prepare our home on the banks of the pond, close to the shore. Our home looks like a pile of wood from the outside. But this should not fool you; we design the inside carefully. First of all, security is of great importance to us. For that is why the only entrance to our home is underwater. Of course, not everyone can easily enter it. We pass through secret tunnels to go in and out.

Karim: This is great. Your house is like a castle surrounded by ditches. It is virtually impossible to enter.

Mr. and Mrs. Beaver laugh at Karim's remark.

You must be asking yourself, "What is this pile of branches in the water for This picture shows the pa of a beaver's house, which is above the surface of the water.

Mr. Beaver: The tunnel leads to an inside chamber. We ensure that this chamber is above the water level. Our family lives in this dry, secure chamber. Sometimes we build two-storey houses, in which the entrance and living room are on the first floor, and the dining room and bedroom on the second. The houses we build have two underwater entrances and a ventilation channel on the top. In this way, besides being secure from exterior dangers, we also live in comfort.

Karim: This is a marvellous thing. It does not appear to have a lodge beneath; it looks as if it is merely a pile of logs and branches. This is surely a remarkable arrangement. I have another question: what is the depth of this pond? From here it looks quite deep.

Mr. Beaver: It is sometimes as deep as 3 or 4 metres. Actually, we don't need such deep water to build our homes. But the surface of the pond freezes in winter and a thick layer of ice forms over it. If the water is not deep enough, the freezing progresses downwards until the entire pond freezes solid. Of course, in that case, we would not be able to move around in the pond. So we deepen the pond as much as possible. Then even if the surface freezes, there is still a layer of water at the bottom of the pond, which is sufficient for us to move and feed in.

Imran: You see, Karim. Mr. and Mrs. Beaver know very well what they are doing. If we were to build a home in the lake, maybe none of these details would occur to us. But our friends think ahead and work at what to do. Surely it is Allah who equips them with the talents to consider such fine details and teaches them what they should do.

43

Beavers swim through a tunnel to enter their lodge. Only beavers know about this tunnel.

Beavers are very intelligent animals. When their lodge is damaged, they realize it at once and repair it, as seen in the picture on the right.

Preparing for winter is another demonstration of the intelligence of beavers. Even if the lodge is covered with snow or the surface of the pond freezes, beavers live in their homes in comfort thanks to the precautions they took in advance.

Once again Karim thinks about his sister, who, as you already know, is a civil engineer. She has had years of education and has worked hard to be an engineer. Karim remembers the day when he went to her room and looked at her school work. Until then he had thought that she had been drawing things like buildings, bridges, etc. He was surprised when he saw her work and could not understand anything. What she was doing was very demanding, difficult and complicated. There were so many lines and figures on the paper that he could not even understand what they signified. He asked his sister what they were, and was amazed when he learned that a building would be built according to these drawings.

Until that day, Karim had not thought that civil engineering could be so difficult. Besides, his sister had told him that she was merely dealing with the design of the building. In the following stages, workers would come into play and would build the building, using various tools and materials.

Karim: This is very interesting. You build your home according to a plan previously made just as Zainab does. Every single thing you do shows great wisdom. I remember my sister working hard for hours making those complicated calculations...

Imran: You are right. I think about Zainab too. But our little friends do the hard work of workers as well as what Zainab does. This also shows the awesome skills Allah has granted to them. However, little friends, it's time for us to go back to the camp now. Thank you very much for everything. You've given us answers to all the questions Karim was curious about. Now we must say good-bye.

Karim: I'd like to thank you, too. I've enjoyed our chat a lot. But I don't want to say good-bye. I'd like to visit you frequently, if you don't mind.

Mr. and Mrs. Beaver: Bye-bye, Karim. Of course you may visit us whenever you wish. You may want to see our house completed. Bye-bye.

Karim is amazed by the tasks these pretty beavers carry out. Now that his questions have been answered, he wants to return to the camp to tell others about what he has learnt.

It is Allah Who created beavers

So you've learnt about beavers along with Karim. As you've seen, thanks to skills possessed at birth, these new friends of Karim can design buildings, which is in fact quite a difficult and complicated task. Then they carry out this plan with great skill. Unlike Karim's sister, beavers do not go to school, nor are they trained for years. But they know exactly what to do, because there is a Supreme Being Who teaches them all these things. This being is Allah, Who created everything, including us.

Remember! A beaver could not have acquired the skill to build dams by chance. It could not have made its body just right for its needs. It could not have discovered by itself the shape to build the dams so that they should be strong enough to withstand the water pressure. And more importantly, it could not have ensured other beavers' possessing the same skills.

There is one more point to note: Beavers could not live if even one of the features they possess were lacking. For example let's consider their teeth. If their back teeth, though not worn down, kept growing like the

Whenever you read
a book or watch a
film about animals,
remember that they
have been created
by Allah.

incisor front teeth, they would become too large, would apply pressure on the jaw and make it impossible for the beaver to use its mouth.

How would the beaver gnaw trees and build dams in this case? How would it build its home? Of course it would not be able to do any of these things. It would not even be able to feed because of the structure of its mouth, so it would eventually starve to death.

Moreover, many organs other than its teeth are especially created for the tasks they perform. Transparent eyelids to protect its eyes when under water as well as special mechanisms that close its ears and nostrils to keep water out are special features which beavers have. Besides these, a beaver has webbed back feet and a stiff, flat tail, which help make the animal a powerful swimmer. These are all advantageous features a beaver has at birth.

You must have understood now why Karim has been so amazed by his little friends.

Karim's little friends possess this body structure, and knowledge and skills to construct dams at birth. All beavers build their homes with Allah's guidance and act in accordance with what He has "inspired" them to do. It is Almighty Allah Who has created these creatures and given them these superior skills.

Allah created all living things with the features that are most appropriate for the tasks they carry out and that fully meet their requirements.

Allah is compassionate to all beings. As Allah states in the Qur'an:

Your god is Allah alone, there is no god but Him. He encompasses all things in His knowledge. (Surah Ta Ha:98)

...Glory be to You! We have no knowledge except what You have taught us. You are the All-Knowing, the All-Wise.

(Surat al-Baqara: 32)

OTHER CHILDREN'S BOOKS BY HARUN YAHYA

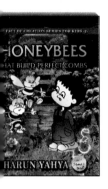
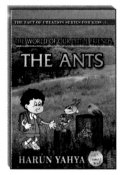
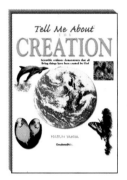
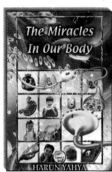

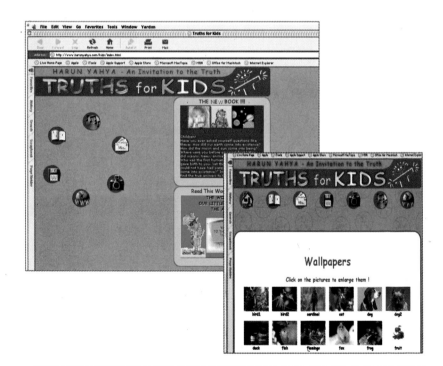

Karim's little friends possess this body structure, and knowledge and skills to construct dams at birth. All beavers build their homes with Allah's guidance and act in accordance with what He has "inspired" them to do. It is Almighty Allah Who has created these creatures and given them these superior skills.

Allah created all living things with the features that are most appropriate for the tasks they carry out and that fully meet their requirements.

Allah is compassionate to all beings. As Allah states in the Qur'an:

Your god is Allah alone, there is no god but Him. He encompasses all things in His knowledge. (Surah Ta Ha:98)

...Glory be to You! We have no knowledge except what You have taught us. You are the All-Knowing, the All-Wise.

(Surat al-Baqara: 32)

OTHER CHILDREN'S BOOKS BY HARUN YAHYA

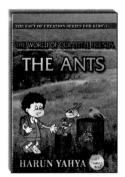

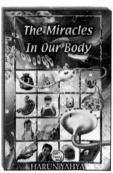

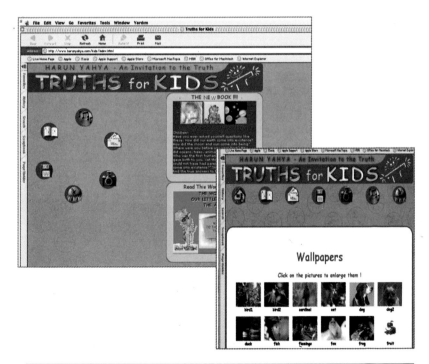